CONCERT FAVORITES

Volume 1

Band Arrangements Correlated with
Essential Elements Band Method Book 1

ISBN 978-0-634-05210-1

7777 W. BLUEMOUND RD. P.O. BOX 13819 MILWAUKEE, WI 53213

00860130

2

LET'S ROCK!

TROMBONE

MICHAEL SWEENEY (ASCAP)

MAJESTIC MARCH

TROMBONE

By PAUL LAVENDER

00860130

MICKEY MOUSE MARCH
(From Walt Disney's "THE MICKEY MOUSE CLUB")

TROMBONE

Words and Music by **JIMMIE DODD**
Arranged by **MICHAEL SWEENEY**

POWER ROCK

(We Will Rock You • Another One Bites The Dust)

TROMBONE

Moderate Rock

"We Will Rock You"

Arranged by MICHAEL SWEENEY

00860130

WHEN THE SAINTS GO MARCHING IN

Words by KATHERINE E. PURVIS
Music by JAMES M. BLACK
Arranged by JOHN HIGGINS

TROMBONE

FARANDOLE
(From "L'Arlésienne")

TROMBONE

GEORGES BIZET
Arranged by MICHAEL SWEENEY (ASCAP)

00860130

8

JUS' PLAIN BLUES

TROMBONE

MICHAEL SWEENEY (ASCAP)

From the Paramount and Twentieth Century Fox Motion Picture TITANIC

MY HEART WILL GO ON

(Love Theme From 'Titanic')

Music by JAMES HORNER
Lyric by WILL JENNINGS
Arranged by PAUL LAVENDER

TROMBONE

Moderately

00860130

From THE MUPPET MOVIE

THE RAINBOW CONNECTION

Words and Music by PAUL WILLIAMS
and KENNITH L. ASCHER
Arranged by PAUL LAVENDER

TROMBONE

From Walt Disney's MARY POPPINS

SUPERCALIFRAGILISTICEXPIALIDOCIOUS

Words and Music by
RICHARD M. SHERMAN and ROBERT B. SHERMAN
Arranged by MICHAEL SWEENEY

TROMBONE

00860130

(From "THE SOUND OF MUSIC")
DO-RE-MI

TROMBONE

Lyrics by OSCAR HAMMERSTEIN II
Music by RICHARD RODGERS
Arranged by PAUL LAVENDER

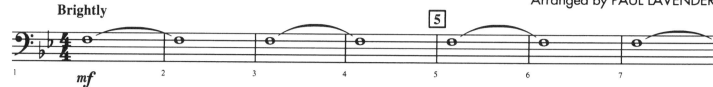

DRUMS OF CORONA

TROMBONE

MICHAEL SWEENEY (ASCAP)

00860130

LAREDO
(Concert March)

TROMBONE

JOHN HIGGINS

POMP AND CIRCUMSTANCE
March No. 1

TROMBONE

By EDWARD ELGAR
Arranged by MICHAEL SWEENEY

Majestically

1. Optional repeat to measure 5

2. Optional repeat to measure 29

3.

00860130

STRATFORD MARCH

TROMBONE

JOHN HIGGINS (ASCAP)

00860130